℮ CELEBRATING ℘

A Christ-Centered

CHRISTMAS

Seven Traditions to
Lead Us Closer to the Savior

EMILY BELLE FREEMAN

ENSIGN PEAK

SALT LAKE CITY, UTAH

For Lisa,
because you asked,
and for Carolyn,
because you remembered

Text © 2010 Emily Belle Freeman

Illustrations © 2010 Jay Bryant Ward

Visit us at EnsignPeakPublishing.com

Library of Congress Cataloging-in-Publication Data
Freeman, Emily, 1969– author.
    Celebrating a Christ-centered Christmas : seven traditions to lead us closer to the Savior / Emily Belle Freeman.
        pages cm
    Includes bibliographical references.
    ISBN 978-1-60907-899-7 (paperbound)
1. Christmas. 2. Jesus Christ—Nativity. I. Title.
    BV45.F73 2014
    232.92—dc23   2014016340

Printed in the United States of America
R. R. Donnelley, Crawfordsville, IN

10   9   8   7   6   5   4   3   2   1

CONTENTS

. . . *the angel said to them, "Do not be afraid; for behold,*
I bring you good news of great joy which will be for all
the people; for today in the city of David there has been born
for you a Savior, who is Christ the Lord."

Luke 2:10–11, NASB

INTRODUCTION

December had come. The house was decorated, most of the presents bought, and Megan and I were driving in the car listening to Christmas carols. Strapped into her car seat and bundled up in her winter coat, Megan did her best to sing along. Then, just as one song ended and another began, Megan said one simple sentence that forever changed the way our family celebrates Christmas. "Mom," she began, "*I* believe in Santa Claus, and *you* believe in Jesus Christ."

It was a moment of epiphany. I thought back over all of our holiday preparations and the experiences we had created for our children. We had written letters to Santa, had talked about being good for Santa, and had counted down the days until Santa would come. We had spent the majority of the season teaching our children to believe in the reality of Santa Claus, and because of our efforts they trusted that he really would come. But suddenly I realized that we had not spent the same amount of time teaching them to believe in the reality of the Savior. I thought over all of the traditions that filled our holiday season and realized that none of them strengthened my children's belief in Jesus Christ.

Since that moment, our home has been transformed into a home that believes. Not only in the magic of Santa, but also in the reality of our Savior, Jesus Christ, who is the true reason behind our celebration. The symbols of Christmas that fill our home throughout the holidays include images that are familiar to all of us—evergreen wreaths, stockings hung by the fire, candy canes, and the magical sound of a bell that still rings. But there is one decoration that has become a family favorite. As the season begins, we place a wooden stable in the center of our family room table. It sits empty, waiting patiently for our Christmas celebrations to begin.

Over the years we have added seven nativity traditions to our holiday celebrations. Inspired from each figure in the nativity set, these traditions have deepened the Christmas spirit that fills our home. Between Thanksgiving and Christmas we set aside seven specific evenings—one for each figure in the nativity. On that evening we spend time learning about the important role that person played in the miracles that surrounded Christ's birth. Then we participate in a simple tradition that reminds us what we can learn from that person's experience. Each of the figures has a story to tell, and each has a lesson to share. Studying their experiences has given our family a greater understanding and a deeper appreciation for the miracles that surround the birth of Christ.

At the end of the evening, after the tradition has been completed, one person from our family is chosen to add the figurine we studied to our nativity scene. Week by week we begin to fill the waiting stable, one figure at a time, until finally the nativity is complete. In the weeks that lead up to Christmas, my children love to watch the nativity come together, almost like an advent counting down to Christmas, and I have noticed that something magical begins to happen: as each figure takes its place within the stable, our hearts are drawn closer to Jesus. The Christ child is always last, placed carefully in the center of the crèche on Christmas morning before we open our gifts.

Within the pages of this book you will discover the lessons and traditions associated with each of the figures in the nativity. The simple traditions that accompany these figures will give you an opportunity to escape from the hustle and bustle of the Christmas season just for a moment as you spend time reflecting on the Savior and the miracle of His birth. You might choose to do these traditions in seven days, or you might start on the Sunday before Thanksgiving and do the traditions for seven weeks. The order of the traditions and the length of time between each one is left completely to your inspiration. Invite anyone you choose to celebrate these moments with you. The stories and traditions are appropriate for any age and families of any size.

The purpose of this book is not to add something more to an already packed holiday season—it is to add something different. The traditions within this book are simple, and you may find that you can combine them with something you already do. Or, maybe you would like to replace one of your current traditions with one that you find in this book. Just as you prepare your home for the holidays, perhaps this year you could take some time to prepare your heart. You might find it helpful to set aside a quiet moment to read through this book before your Christmas celebrations begin. Perhaps you would like to highlight certain passages to share aloud on the evening you celebrate each tradition. As you read you will quickly discover that the chapters of this book can be done in any order—this will allow you to decide what will work best for your circumstances.

This is a season of anticipation and celebration, and hopefully you will let those two emotions become the guiding principles for your holiday experience: anticipation for a Christmas filled with the Spirit of Christ, and celebration in honor of the miracle of His birth.

May this holiday season be one of your fondest in recent years, and may your heart be filled with the Christmas spirit that only He can bring.

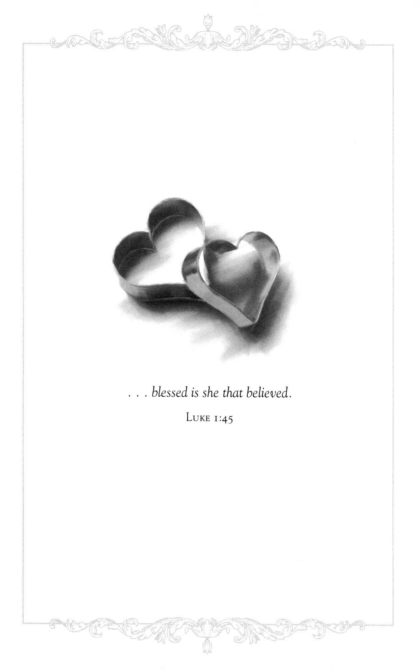

. . . blessed is she that believed.

Luke 1:45

MARY

There are no words to adequately describe a mother's heart at Christmas, nor the thoughts that are pondered within. As the season approaches there are so many meaningful details that must be taken care of and arrangements to be made. Part of the holiday preparation includes pondering moments—every mother wants every part of Christmas to be *just* right. We agonize over the perfect gifts; we contemplate how to create lasting memories; and we long for meaningful celebrations. These reflective moments are a familiar part of Christmas for every mother and are poignantly described in the following story.

♦ ♦ ♦

THE WIDOW'S MIGHT
Elaine Stirland McKay

Bessie watched the wind hurl snow as it howled through Huntsville, Utah. It's a cold Christmas Eve, she thought, colder than those of the Depression . . . colder now that her husband was dead.

Before the fire had flickered out, Bessie had heated the iron and made her way up the winding stairs of the stone home to iron the sheets before her eight children climbed into their beds.

"Warmmm," purred the baby as she snuggled in her crib. Even Bessie's sixteen-year-old son chuckled and sighed as his feet found where the iron had been. The children were noisily unaware that the iron was heated by bits of slack coal from a supply that wouldn't last the winter. Nor had they ever noticed that the smiling woman who pressed the sheets wore patched dresses and was somehow never hungry.

The next morning Bessie would build the

fire while the four boys went out to feed and milk old Sally, the only animal not sold to pay debts. The little girls would wait in the kitchen until chores were done. Then all would line up—smallest to tallest—and, at the sound of Bessie's first notes on the piano, would march and sing their way in to the tree: "O come, all ye faithful, joyful and triumphant . . ."

They had cut the tree themselves and trimmed it with paper chains and popcorn. But there was nothing under it, and Bessie had little to put there. Someone had sent her a few oranges and nuts. That was enough, she knew, to cause shouts of delight. But, as she sat looking out at the half-buried village, the old question returned, "What can I give my children for Christmas?" After a moment she saw the answer.

In the morning when songs were sung and oranges eaten, Bessie said, "Today, because it's Christmas Day, we're going to do something special. We are going to take gifts to a family who is poor." The house grew quiet. Poor was a word they shunned.

Then Bessie, her eyes shining, explained that many people in the world had very little and, since they themselves had so much, it was only right that they share. They could look through their possessions and find a gift—a hair ribbon, a book, some clothes . . . "And I'll make apple pies," she beamed.

When the pies were cooled, Bessie placed two in a basket where the children had put their gifts. She covered all with a bright cloth. At last everything was ready. Then above the excited chatter, a boy's voice demanded, "Mother, why are we doing this when we don't have enough for ourselves?"

There. Someone had said it. The smiles vanished. Even the baby was silent.

"What we have is enough," Bessie said softly, "and what we are giving is small. We are keeping the precious things . . . this great stone house built by your grandfather, our love for one another, happy memories of what has been, hope for good things that are to come. . . . All this is ours to keep. These few gifts we have gathered are ours to share. Come, my son, you may carry the basket."

Christmas night was cold, and Bessie again ironed the sheets. Amid the clamor of getting ready for bed, she felt a sense of peace and assurance. She could not know that one of her sons would become a United States congressman and one, a United States federal judge, or that all of her sons would serve in the armed services protecting freedom around the world. She could not visualize the twelve college degrees, the scholarships, trophies, and awards that would accumulate. She could not foresee the shared planning, pennies, and prayers that would cause it all to happen. And later that evening as she watched the last ember die in the old stove and felt the house grow cold, she little knew that in twenty-seven years she would be named Utah's Mother of the Year.

Bessie knew only that she had given her children something for Christmas that they could never lose. Years from now on a cold winter night when they were far from home, they would find it, small and sacred, in their hearts. And there would be other things she could give to them as days and months went by—little things—like warmed sheets.[1]

◆　◆　◆

I often wonder, when my children are far from home, what Christmas memories they will hold, small and sacred, in their hearts. There is one memory that I hope they will never forget—it is a memory made year after year in our family room. I begin decorating for Christmas on November first. I can't help it—I love being surrounded by the holiday. Many years ago I started a new Christmas decorating tradition: one room in our house is devoted entirely to Jesus. This room is filled with nativities from all over the world. The Christmas tree ornaments are stars of all different shapes and sizes. I love this room, especially at night when I turn out all of the lights in our home just before bed. Then, with just the Christmas tree to cast a soft glow on the manger scenes that fill the room, I sit and ponder the true meaning of Christmas. Most winter evenings find me wrapped in a blanket on the couch in this room, even if it is just for a few minutes. Sometimes my husband, Greg, or one of my children will join me. These are small, sacred moments in the midst of our celebrations—moments I hope my children will forever remember. I love these pondering moments.

When I look at a nativity scene my heart is always

drawn to Mary, the handmaiden of the Lord. The testimony of Luke is filled with scriptures that help us to understand more about the kind of woman Mary was. In the first chapter of Luke we read that Mary had found favor with God (v. 30), and that the Lord was with her (v. 28). The scriptures also tell us that she was blessed among women. At the very end of the first chapter of Luke we are given a rare privilege—we have the opportunity to hear Mary's unwavering testimony, pure and strong, straight from her heart. Mary said, "My soul doth magnify the Lord, and my spirit hath rejoiced in God my Saviour. . . . for he that is mighty hath done to me great things; and holy is his name. . . . He hath shewed strength with his arm; . . . He hath filled the hungry with good things; . . . He hath holpen his servant Israel . . ." (Luke 1:46–54).

Mary was a remarkable woman who magnified the Lord and who rejoiced in her knowledge of the Christ. She recognized the tender mercies and the great things that filled her life. She knew God's strength and His holiness. She testified of the good things that come from devotion to Him.

At the very end of the account of the first Christmas night found in Luke 2 there is one scripture that tugs on my heartstrings. After the events of the evening died down and the parade of visitors had left the stable "Mary kept all these things, and pondered them in her heart" (Luke 2:19). Mary spent the first Christmas doing what every mother does—she pondered.

Have you ever wondered what it was that Mary pondered? Surely she must have reflected, just like all new mothers do, on the baby's tiny fingers and wrinkled, newborn feet. Her thoughts were probably caught up in the wonder of the recent delivery and the miracle of birth. Somewhere there must have been gratitude for the blessing of finally finding a quiet place to deliver the Son of God, even if that setting was rustic and simple. Perhaps she thought of her overwhelming love for a loyal husband who had stood by her through so much. And as humble strangers sent by angels filled that rustic stable, did she long for the familiarity of family and friends who normally would have been there to support and sustain her?

I imagine Mary's heart was full to almost bursting on

that night. Thoughts of wonder, contentment, and grati-tude must have warmed her heart—celebration for the moment, anticipation for what lay ahead. The blessing. The burden. The responsibility. The gift. As she sat sur-rounded by heaven's hosts, humble strangers, a devoted husband, and the shelter of unexpected circumstance, I wonder if Isaiah's prophecy filled her heart: "For unto us a child is born, unto us a son is given . . . and his name shall be called Wonderful, Counsellor, The mighty God, The everlasting Father, The Prince of Peace" (Isaiah 9:6).

In my mind's eye, I can see Mary. Her head is turned to one side, and I can see her smile. Her eyes sparkle, and I see the baby nestled within her arms—cherished, protected, content. I am certain that there were moments when Mary held that tiny baby in her arms and pled with the Lord, *This is my child, I am His mother. Give us time to know each other.* I am sure she must have longed for and treasured the quiet moments with her son. Later in that same chapter of Luke we are told that "his mother kept all these sayings in her heart" (Luke 2:51). Oh, the thoughts, emotions, and experiences that must have filled that young mother's heart.

Amid the comings and goings of that first Christmas, I wonder if Mary felt a sense of peace and assurance in her heart: happy memories of what had already taken place, hope for good things that would come. She could not know that her son would one day teach profound lessons from the scriptures to multitudes of people; that men would leave behind their livelihood to follow Him; that His hands would be the means of healing the sick, raising the dead, calming the sea. Nor could she know that one of His closest friends would betray Him; that those who once honored Him would crucify Him; that above all else He would choose to follow His Father's will. She could not visualize the crown of thorns on His head, the nails in His hands, the cross that He would bear. She could not foresee the feelings that would enter her heart in the moment when the tomb was found empty or when the disciples she revered would testify boldly, "He lives." In the stillness of that evening as she watched over her sleeping, swaddled son, she little knew the extent of what was to happen within the next thirty-three years. Mary knew only what she felt in her heart. Years from that night I wonder if she looked back on that moment, still and sacred, and remembered those thoughts she pondered.

When I think of Mary, I think of her heart. That thought has led to a Christmas tradition that focuses on the importance of heartfelt pondering. It is a tradition that allows me to set aside my reflections over the details, the arrangements, and the planning of the holiday, and spend an evening just like Mary did, pondering the night of Christ's birth.

One of my favorite experiences with this tradition happened many years ago. After a night of caroling with several teenagers in our neighborhood, we gathered together in a nearby home. We sang "Silent Night" and then talked about what it meant to ponder, just like Mary had, the events of the night Jesus was born. Then we asked each person in the room to think about this question, "If you had been there on the night of Christ's birth, who would you have wanted to be, and why?"

The answers were thought provoking. Some chose

to be Joseph, the protector, and some Mary, because they longed to hold the baby. Still others chose the angels bringing joy, or the shepherds, because they chose to testify of Christ. There was even one boy who chose the cow, because he gave up his bed and shared his stable, giving all he had for the Lord.

As each person around the room shared his or her thoughts, the spirit of Christmas entered our hearts and we thought about what it would have been like to have been there, in Bethlehem, on the night the Savior was born. I learned a great lesson from Mary, and it is one that continues in our home today—one night of the season is devoted to pondering the night of Christ's birth in our hearts.

PONDER

A Christmas Hymn

"Silent Night"

A Story to Tell . . . A Lesson to Share

Read Luke 1:26–56 and Luke 2:5–7, 19

What do these verses teach about Mary's character? As you read each scripture, focus on what was most important to her. Take a moment to consider what Mary might have pondered in her heart.

The Moment of Celebration

Spend an evening learning about Mary and what she might have pondered in her heart. You could bake and decorate heart-shaped sugar cookies to snack on. It might be fun to make paper cutout hearts with scrapbook supplies to hang on your tree. Set aside time to reflect on your thoughts of the night of Christ's birth. If you could have been anyone present on the first Christmas night, who would you choose to be, and why? Share your thoughts with others or take a moment to write them down. Ponder what the birth of the Savior means to you. Once you have finished, place the figure of Mary in your nativity scene.

MARY

reminds us that we need to find a moment
to ponder the events of that sacred night in Bethlehem.
In that moment we celebrate the miracle of Christ's birth,
and the gift that heaven gave.

Joseph her husband . . . a just man.

Matthew 1:19

two

JOSEPH

The real story of Christmas begins with a young man and his weary wife who were desperately searching for somewhere to stay. When I look at the figure of Joseph in my nativity set I find myself wondering what emotions filled his soul in those final moments that led up to the birth of Jesus. The early events of that evening must have been heartbreaking for Joseph, the protector and guardian of his tiny family, as he watched the woman he loved entering into labor without a place to stay.

The scriptures tell us that on that night "there was no room for them in the inn" (Luke 2:7). It seems logical that the young couple did not just stop at one place to find shelter, but were turned away over and over again with the words that must have become discouragingly familiar, "no room."

Our Christmas season sometimes resembles that first Christmas night. The season is packed so full that we may find ourselves echoing that same sentiment, "no room." With parties and programs, shopping and decorating, it is hard to make room for anything extra. But after the last gift is given, the fancy dishes are cleared away, and the house is finally settled down for an evening, how often do we find ourselves longing for something more?

It is in those quiet hours that I think of Joseph. On that first Christmas night there was no room, only the shelter of a small, simple stable. It was in that humble circumstance that the Savior was born. I often wonder, as I think of Joseph caring for his weary wife, if he watched over the newborn child and longed for family, a warm meal, a soft bed for his wife, and a handmade blanket for the baby.

For our family, it is the thought of this humble setting

that has led to a special tradition filled with service. Not just any service, but heartfelt service. Secret acts of kindness, given to those who are desperately in need. The type of service described in this familiar Christmas story.

◆ ◆ ◆

A Gift from the Heart
Norman Vincent Peale

New York City, where I live, is impressive at any time, but as Christmas approaches, it's overwhelming. Store windows blaze with light and color, furs and jewels. Golden angels, 40 feet tall, hover over Fifth Avenue. Wealth, power, opulence—nothing in the world can match this fabulous display.

Through the gleaming canyons, people hurry to find last-minute gifts. Money seems to be no problem. If there's a problem, it's that the recipients so often have everything they need or want that it's hard to find anything suitable, anything that will really say, "I love you."

Last December, as Christ's birthday drew near, a stranger was faced with just that problem. She had come from Switzerland to live in an American home and perfect her English. In return, she was willing to act as secretary, mind the grandchildren, do anything that was asked. She was just a girl in her late teens. Her name was Ursula.

One of the tasks her employers gave Ursula was keeping track of Christmas presents as they arrived. There were many, and all would require acknowledgment. Ursula kept a faithful record, but with a growing concern. She was grateful to her American friends; she wanted to show her gratitude by giving them a Christmas present. But nothing that she could buy with her small allowance could compare with the gifts she was recording daily. Besides, even without these gifts, it seemed that her employers already had everything.

At night, from her window, Ursula could see the snowy expanse of Central Park, and beyond it the jagged skyline of the city. Far below, in the restless streets, taxis hooted and traffic lights winked red and green. It was so different from the silent majesty of the Alps that at times she had to blink back tears of the homesickness she was careful never to show. It was in the solitude of her little room, a few days before Christmas, that a secret idea came to Ursula.

It was almost as if a voice spoke clearly, inside her head. "It's true," said the voice, "that many people in this city have much more than you do. But surely there are many who have far less. If you will think about this, you may find a solution to what's troubling you."

Ursula thought long and hard. Finally on her day off, which was Christmas Eve, she went to a great department store. She moved slowly along the crowded aisles, selecting and rejecting things in her mind. At last she bought something, and had it wrapped in gaily colored paper. She went out into the gray twilight and looked helplessly around. Finally, she went up to a doorman, resplendent in blue and gold. "Excuse me, please," she said in her hesitant English, "can you tell me where to find a poor street?"

"A poor street, miss?" said the puzzled man.

"Yes, a very poor street. The poorest in the city."

The doorman looked doubtful. "Well, you might try Harlem. Or down in the Village. Or the Lower East Side, maybe."

But these names meant nothing to Ursula.

She thanked the doorman and walked along, threading her way through the stream of shoppers until she came to a tall policeman. "Please," she said, "can you direct me to a very poor street . . . in Harlem?"

The policeman looked at her sharply and shook his head. "Harlem's no place for you, miss." And he blew his whistle and sent the traffic swirling past.

Holding her package carefully, Ursula walked on, head bowed against the sharp wind. If a street looked poorer than the one she was on, she took it. But none seemed like the slums she had heard about. Once she stopped a woman, "Please, where do the very poor people live?" But the woman gave her a hard stare and hurried on.

Darkness came sifting from the sky. Ursula was cold and discouraged and afraid of becoming lost. She came to an intersection and stood forlornly on the corner. What she was trying to do suddenly seemed foolish, impulsive, absurd. Then, through the traffic's roar, she heard the cheerful tinkle of a bell. On the corner opposite, a Salvation Army man was making his holiday traditional Christmas appeal.

At once Ursula felt better; The Salvation Army was a part of life in Switzerland, too. Surely this man could tell her what she wanted to know. She waited for the light, then crossed over to him. "Can you help me? I'm looking for a baby. I have here a little present for the poorest baby I can find." And she held up the package with the green ribbon and the gaily colored paper.

Dressed in gloves and overcoat a size too big for him, he seemed a very ordinary man. But behind his steel-rimmed glasses his eyes were kind. He looked at Ursula and stopped ringing his bell. "What sort of present?" he asked.

"A little dress. For a small, poor baby. Do you know of one?"

"Oh, yes," he said. "Of more than one, I'm afraid."

"Is it far away? I could take a taxi maybe?"

The Salvation Army man wrinkled his forehead. Finally he said, "It's almost six o'clock. My relief will show up then. If you want to wait, and you can afford a dollar taxi ride, I'll take you to a family in my own neighborhood who needs just about everything."

"And they have a small baby?"

"A very small baby."

"Then," said Ursula joyfully, "I wait!"

The substitute bell-ringer came. A cruising taxi slowed. In its welcome warmth, she told her new friend about herself, how she came to be in New York, what she was trying to do. He listened in silence, and the taxi driver listened too. When they reached their destination, the driver said, "Take your time, miss. I'll wait for you." On the sidewalk, Ursula stared up at the forbidding tenement—dark, decaying, saturated with hopelessness. A gust of wind, iron-cold, stirred the refuse in the street and rattled the reeling ash cans. "They live on the third floor," the Salvation Army man said. "Shall we go up?"

But Ursula shook her head. "They would try to thank me, and this is not from me." She pressed the package into his hand. "Take it up for me, please. Say it's from . . . from someone who has everything."

The taxi bore her swiftly from the dark streets to lighted ones, from misery to abundance. She tried to visualize the Salvation Army man climbing the stairs, the knock, the explanation, the package being opened, the dress on the baby. It was hard to do.

Arriving at the apartment on Fifth Avenue where she lived, she fumbled in her purse. But the driver flicked the flag up. "No charge, miss."

"No charge?" echoed Ursula, bewildered.

"Don't worry," the driver said. "I've been paid." He smiled at her and drove away.

Ursula was up early the next day. She set the table with special care. By the time she was finished, the family was awake, and there was all the excitement and laughter of Christmas morning. Soon the living room was a sea of gay discarded wrappings. Ursula thanked everyone for the presents she received.

Finally, when there was a lull, she began to explain hesitantly why there seemed to be none from her. She told about going to the department store. She told about the Salvation Army man. She told about the taxi driver. When she was finished, there was a long silence. No one seemed to trust himself to speak.

"So you see," said Ursula, "I try to do kindness in your name. And this is my Christmas present to you."

How do I know all this? I know it because ours was the home where Ursula lived. Ours was the Christmas she shared. We were like many

Americans, so richly blessed that to this child there seemed to be nothing she could add to all the material things we already had. And so she offered something of far greater value: a gift from the heart, an act of kindness carried out in our name.

Strange, isn't it? A shy Swiss girl, alone in a great impersonal city. You would think that nothing she could do would affect anyone. And yet, by trying to give away love, she brought the true spirit of Christmas into our lives, the spirit of selfless giving. That was Ursula's secret—and she shared it with us all.[2]

◆ ◆ ◆

One of my favorite parts of this story is that in the midst of the traffic's roar, Ursula heard the cheerful tinkle of a bell. Such a quiet noise in the midst of confusion, but through the cacophony of sound, Ursula heard the tiny bell ring. Because she followed its sound, she was eventually led to someone who needed what she had to give.

If we choose, we too can hear the silent promptings amidst the holiday confusion—whispers of what we might do to share an act of kindness with someone in need this season. Ursula's gift was powerful because she performed an act of kindness in someone else's name. Her journey to make sure the present ended up where it was really needed increased the meaning of the gift.

One afternoon in 1999 my three-year-old daughter, Megan, and I were watching the news. There was a segment that caught my attention. It was the week before Christmas and the Salvation Army was struggling to fill their little red buckets. Where normally they would have gathered 950,000 dollars, this year they had received only 200,000 dollars. We wanted to do something to help, so throughout the rest of the week we set out a bowl on the table to collect all of our spare change. Megan's job was to remember to fill her pockets with change from the bowl every time we left the house. She spent the last week of Christmas filling up the little red buckets everywhere we went. I will never forget the image I have of three-year-old Megan that year: the careful way she listened for the familiar ringing of the bell, her pockets stuffed with pennies, dimes, and nickels, her fingers fumbling to make sure each coin made it into the bucket. To this day, whenever Megan hears the tinkling bell, she likes to put money in the little red buckets of the Salvation Army.

Can you hear the cheerful tinkle of the bell this season? What is it prompting you to do? Perhaps you will deliver a festively wrapped gift to someone in need. You could make a blanket for someone who is lonely, or drop off hats and gloves to a homeless shelter. Maybe you could prepare a turkey dinner and have it delivered anonymously to a family that is struggling financially.

The tradition of the tinkling bell suggests a whispered prompting that might be followed and an act of secret service that could be performed. A familiar Christmas quote counsels, "At one time most of my friends could hear the bell, but as years passed, it fell silent for all of them. Though I've grown old, the bell still rings for me as it does for all who truly believe."[3] In a season that is packed full with the hustle and bustle of Christmas, I hope each of us will make room in our hearts to hear the tinkling bell and live as true believers. Spend some time this week opening your heart to hear the quiet prompt-ings. Maybe you could stick a small bell into one of your pockets. As you hear its cheerful sound throughout the day it could act as a reminder for you to follow a quiet prompting and perform a secret act of kindness. The ser-vice might require you to journey out of your way, but I have found that often the journey that accompanies the giving of these heartfelt gifts becomes one of my most precious Christmas memories.

Over the years other families have joined us in fol-lowing the quiet promptings that accompany the tra-dition of the bell. One family was worried about the difficulty of sending Christmas gifts to their parents who were living in a foreign country. They gathered together at the beginning of December with all of the children and grandchildren and extended an invitation to each family member to participate in a secret act of service. Then they sent an e-mail to their parents and told them to watch for an e-mail from each of their children and grandchildren, with instructions that they weren't to open the e-mails until Christmas morning. The e-mail letters would become their gift—an act of service performed in their name. Within the next few weeks the couple received over twenty-five e-mails from their family. On Christmas Day they shared the e-mail letters describing the acts of service. Each heartfelt experience became a treasured gift.

I like to think that if I had been in Bethlehem on that first Christmas night I would have brought a warm meal and a handmade blanket in celebration of the new birth. Listening for the cheerful tinkling of the bell and then following the quiet promptings to serve in the midst of our celebrations has become our family's way of realizing that heartfelt desire. Over the years I have noticed that somehow the service and the sacrifice have become part of the gift, and I have come to believe that when a gift requires great sacrifice it becomes more precious, both to the giver and to the one who receives.

SERVE

A Christmas Hymn

"Away in a Manger"

A Story to Tell . . . A Lesson to Share

Read Matthew 1:18–25 and Luke 2:1–7

Take a moment to consider what it must have felt like when Joseph realized that there was no room in the inn. What would you have offered Joseph and his family if you had been there? How can performing secret acts of service help to make room for the Savior in our hearts today? Does Joseph remind you of someone you know who is in need this Christmas season?

The Moment of Celebration

Read "A Gift from the Heart."

Talk about the promptings that can come to us even

when we are surrounded by the confusion of the holidays. Can you hear the tinkling bell? What gift of service is it prompting you to give? Take some time to come up with a plan for your secret act of service. Here are several suggestions you might try.

- Try carrying a small bell in one of your pockets every day this week. Let its sound become a quiet reminder to listen for promptings that will allow you to serve someone secretly every day.

- Purchase a large jingle bell to be passed around your family. Secretly ask one person in your family to start the tradition. Have them perform a secret act of kindness for another family member. When they are finished they should place the bell on the pillow of the person they served.

  If the bell is on your pillow you get to perform the next secret act of kindness and then leave the bell on the pillow of the person you served. Let the tradition continue all week long.

- Perform an act of kindness that will require help from the whole family and can be done in one evening.

Maybe there is a service you can perform for a specific person in your neighborhood.

- Get involved in a "Sub for Santa" program. You might pick a family to help who has children similar in age to those in your family.

- Visit someone who is sick, or stop by a rest home and deliver homemade sugar cookies or Christmas cards. Christmas is a particularly lonely time for many people. Your family could make a big difference to them.

- One Christmas our family delivered several food baskets—each containing a ham, potatoes, canned corn, rolls, candy canes, and a brownie mix—to several families in need.

- Gather clothing to take to a homeless shelter, or collect up and refurbish old toys to donate to a thrift store.

Once you are finished celebrating your tinkling bell tradition, write down the service that you gave and the journey you took to make sure the act of service got to the right place. Include any important details you don't want to forget. You might consider starting a tinkling bell journal to record these secret acts of kindness. Leave it in a prominent place where members of your family can record their experiences all through the Christmas season. Over the years this journal will become a treasured keepsake.

Once you have accomplished your act of service, you can place the figure of Joseph in your nativity scene.

JOSEPH

represents the desires of our hearts.
He reminds us of the secret acts of Christmas kindness
given with sacrifice and love
to the broken, the weary, the lost, or the lonely.

*Fear not . . . I bring you good
tidings of great joy.*

LUKE 2:10

three

THE ANGEL

There is a certain feeling that surrounds the Christmas season—every day is filled with anticipation of good things to come. We prepare delicious food together in the kitchen, hide behind closed doors wrapping gifts, and make plans to gather with family and friends. As we count down the days from the first to the twenty-fourth, the feeling of expectation grows. I find it interesting how much this feeling of anticipation reminds me of the simple gift the angels brought to the shepherds on that first Christmas night—good tidings and great joy.

In my mind's eye, I can picture the angels hovering

over the shepherd's field in a magical moment when "heaven and earth seemed to mingle, as suddenly an Angel stood before their dazzled eyes, while the out-streaming glory of the Lord seemed to enwrap them, as in a mantle of light. Surprise, awe, fear would be hushed into calm and expectancy as from the Angel they heard . . . the great joy of those good tidings which he brought: that the long-promised Saviour, Messiah, Lord, was born in the City of David. . . .

"It was as if attendant angels had only waited the signal. . . . Heaven took up the strain of 'glory'; earth echoed it as 'peace'; it fell on the ears and hearts of men as 'good pleasure':

> "Glory to God in the highest—
> And upon earth peace—
> Among men good pleasure!"[4]

I love to imagine the multitude of heaven gathering to fill the night with the emotion that is so much a part of the Christmas season—the anticipation of good things to come.

Have you ever noticed that many of the Christmas carols inspire within us those same feelings of good tidings and great joy? Phillips Brooks, author of "O Little Town of Bethlehem," wrote the following of an experience he had on Christmas Eve in 1865: "I remember especially on Christmas Eve, when I was standing in the old church in Bethlehem, close to the spot where Jesus was born, when the whole church was ringing hour after hour with splendid hymns of praise to God, how again and again it seemed as if I could hear voices I knew well, telling each other of the 'Wonderful Night' of the Savior's birth."[5]

I love the thought of voices we know well, telling each other of the night of Christ's birth. Isn't that what we do when we gather together to sing as friends, families, or congregations? It is one of the sacred ways we testify to each other of the birth of our Savior. Throughout our neighborhoods, from home to home and door to door, voices we know well spread great joy and good tidings with melodies that fill our homes and hearts with the Spirit. The songs help us to picture that first Christmas when the "world in solemn stillness lay to hear the angels sing."[6] "Glories stream from heaven afar, heavenly hosts sing Alleluia,"[7] and within that moment heaven's invitation was extended, the same invitation that calls to us today, "Come and behold Him, . . . O, come, let us adore Him."[8]

Carolers are heaven-sent angels at Christmastime, gathering together to repeat the sounding joy, encouraging every heart to prepare Him room, and echoing the wish nestled inside each of our hearts: "Be near me, Lord Jesus, I ask thee to stay close by me forever, and love me, I pray."[9] Somehow the music softens our hearts, lifts our spirits, and draws us closer to the Lord. The humble invitation of the carolers calls out to each of us: "Come to Bethlehem and see, . . . Come, adore on bended knee."[10] Through them we are led to trust that "where meek souls will receive him, still the dear Christ enters in,"[11] and to find comfort in the promise that the "hopes and fears of all the years"[12] will be met in Him. The hearts of the carolers petition just as ours does, "O come, O come, Emmanuel,"[13] and together we celebrate the joyous tidings given on that first Christmas night—Christ is born in Bethlehem.

Good news. Glad tidings.

Spreading anticipation. Spreading joy.

On that night, over two thousand years ago, the hosts of heaven gathered. Filled with awe and excitement and bursting with emotion, they came to celebrate the moment that had been anticipated since the world began. Knowing what it would mean to the world, the multitude of angels extended the first invitation on that Christmas night to a group of shepherds gathered in a sacred field: Come unto Christ. I imagine they must have watched for the joy on the faces of the shepherds as they ran with haste to the stable to discover the precious gift hidden inside.

Today the invitation is the same. Come. Prepare Him room. Invite Him in. "Where charity stands watching and faith holds wide the door, the dark night wakes, the glory breaks, and Christmas comes once more."[14]

Hold wide the door. Create the anticipation of Christmas by filling your home or your heart with the carols of the season. There are several ways to do this. One way is to invite others to go caroling with you. Spend a night spreading the joy of the season as you travel from door to door caroling. If it is too cold out, spend the evening gathered at home with family or friends around your own Christmas tree singing carols.

If you would prefer a more quiet celebration, perhaps you could try something like this. Gather a collection of Christmas CDs in which each song testifies of Christ. As you listen to the carols, remember the real reason for the celebration and the anticipation contained within. Many evenings find me snuggled up on my couch with a cup of hot cocoa, listening to these familiar voices testify of the birth of Jesus.

It seems that a night of caroling just isn't complete without gathering at home for hot cocoa when you are through. Any cocoa recipe will do, but I will share my favorite with you. It is a French Cocoa recipe I learned from my mother, and Christmas just isn't Christmas without a frothy mug.

FRENCH COCOA

5 (1-ounce) squares unsweetened chocolate

1½ cups sugar

⅔ cup water

4 cups whipped cream

Bring chocolate, sugar, and water to a rolling boil. Boil for 3 minutes, stirring continually. Let chocolate mixture cool to room temperature. Once cooled, fold chocolate mixture into whipped cream. (If chocolate mixture is too solid to fold into the cream, blend ¼ cup of whipped cream into the mixture, then fold chocolate into the cream.)

Refrigerate until use.

To use: Pour ½ cup milk into a mug. Microwave for one minute. Add 3 heaping tablespoons of chilled cocoa mix. Stir. You may need to warm the mug for 15 seconds more.

♦ ♦ ♦

This Christmas season remember the importance of the angels on that first Christmas night and the sweet message they brought to the earth. They came to spread great joy, to give good tidings, to create anticipation. Let the music of this season surround you, and as you listen to familiar voices testify of the Savior's birth, may you find your heart filling with those same emotions, not just until it is full—but until it is overflowing.

SHARE THE JOY

A Christmas Hymn

"O Little Town of Bethlehem"

A Story to Tell . . . A Lesson to Share

Read Luke 2:9–14

What was the great joy and good tidings that the angels brought? What would the news have meant to you if you were there? What does it mean to you today? How does their announcement create feelings of anticipation in your heart? Talk about some of your favorite carols that testify of Christ. Why are they so dear to you? How do they make you feel?

The Moment of Celebration

Spend an evening listening to or singing carols that testify of Christ. Let the great joy and good tidings of the season fill your home and your heart. Find warmth from the message of the melodies. End the evening by enjoying a steaming mug of cocoa. Fill your heart with anticipation. After you finish, place the figure of the angel in your nativity scene.

THE ANGEL

*embodies a heart that runneth over
with the good tidings and great joy of the season.
The angel is a reminder that the anticipation
of good things to come
should fill our hearts with warmth overflowing.*

Let us now go . . . and they came with haste.

Luke 2:15–16

four

THE SHEPHERD

The December I was eight years old, I became very ill. The severity of the illness necessitated that I be quarantined in our house for weeks. To prevent any chance of spreading the illness, I could have no visitors. I missed all of the holiday celebrations—the family gatherings, making candy cane cookies and fudge, going to see the lights.

Now, over thirty years later, there is not much I remember about that Christmas. I don't remember any of the gifts given or received. I must have been immensely sad to miss all of the school celebrations and heartbroken to miss the family gatherings, but even those memories have left me.

What I do know is that every year we gather together to watch our family videos, and when we come to the celebration for the year 1978, I am not there. I missed Christmas. It doesn't matter how many times I watch the video and see the panda pillows my grandma made for each of the grandchildren and the hand-sewn, super-hero capes made for the little boys, I still have no recollection of that experience. I can't remember the moment because I wasn't a part of the celebration—I wasn't there.

When I think of the first Christmas night, my thoughts often focus on the shepherds. Theirs was a twenty-four-hour job. The responsibility of their assignment did not end when the sun went down—they tended the flock all day and their watch care extended through the night. Then came the night when the angel of the Lord visited the shepherds abiding in the field, keeping watch over their flock, and extended an invitation: "For unto you is born this day in the city of David a Saviour, which is Christ the Lord. . . . Ye shall find the babe wrapped in swaddling clothes, lying in a manger" (Luke 2:11–12).

On that important evening, I wonder if each

shepherd accepted the invitation. After the announcement was given, did they *all* go now and with haste to see the thing the Lord had made known unto them?

I like to think they did.

It breaks my heart to think of the opportunity missed if one shepherd hadn't gone. How would it be to live your life knowing you weren't a part of the celebration, that you missed the memory, to know you could never get back the moment because you weren't there? How would it feel to know you missed Christ?

Each of us has the opportunity every Christmas to search for and find the Lord. If we carefully study the story of the shepherds found in Luke 2, we can learn much about what it means to search for the Lord in the midst of the celebration, and the importance of sharing with others what we hear, see, and feel after those experiences. From the example of the shepherds we learn what we need to do to make sure we don't miss Christ within our Christmas celebrations.

Of all the characters in the nativity, the shepherds happen to be my favorite. I come from a long line of shepherds, but that is not what makes them so endearing to me. It is what the shepherds did just after the angels came that has drawn my admiration and respect. Actually, the importance is not necessarily in what they did, but in *how* they did it. The scriptures explain, "And it came to pass, as the angels were gone away from them into heaven, the shepherds said one to another, Let us *now* go even unto Bethlehem, and see this thing which is come to pass, which the Lord hath made known unto us. And they came *with haste*, and found Mary, and Joseph, and the babe lying in a manger" (Luke 2:15–16; emphasis added). I love the words *now* and *with haste*. It is as if the scriptures are telling us that in their excitement to see the Lord the shepherds went immediately—they could not wait. I like to hope that is what I would have done if I had been there.

This part of the Christmas story causes reason for reflection. I often wonder when the invitation to come unto Christ is extended to me, if I have the heart of a shepherd. When given the opportunity to turn to the scriptures, to pray, to learn more of Him, how often is my response *now* and *with haste?* This scripture reminds me of the importance of *desire*. If our hearts are filled with desire to come closer to Christ, it will motivate our actions for good.

I also find great counsel in the part of the scripture that says, "the shepherds said *one to another*, Let *us* now go . . ." (Luke 2:15; emphasis added). Those are the kind of friends I want to surround myself with, ones that will encourage me to go where Jesus is, and who want to accompany me there.

The third lesson we learn from the shepherds is found in verses 17 and 18 (emphasis added): "And when they had seen it, they made known abroad the saying which was told them concerning this child. And *all* they that heard it wondered at those things which were told them by the shepherds." I love that the shepherds did not keep the joy to themselves—instead they shared it! And not just with a few people, the scriptures use the word *all*. The story of the shepherds reminds me of the importance of sharing our testimonies of Christ.

Just as the shepherds made known abroad their testimonies concerning the Lord, we too must find opportunities where we can share what our knowledge of Jesus

Christ means to us. In our search to find Christ within Christmas, the humble sharing of our witness of His hand in our lives can inspire joyful moments of celebration. These sweet moments will allow Christ to be part of our celebrations, to be included in our memories; it will give us an opportunity to make sure we don't miss Christ in the midst of Christmas.

A simple Christmas tradition our children have always loved gives us the opportunity to consider the shepherds and to remember the Savior as we share our witness of Him.

First we spend time together baking candy cane cookies, which represent a shepherd's staff. These fun cookies will fill your home with a sweet Christmas aroma as they bake.

SHEPHERD'S STAFF (CANDY CANE) COOKIES

1 cup sugar
1 cup butter, softened
½ cup milk
1 egg
3½ cups flour
1 teaspoon baking powder

¼ *teaspoon salt*
1 teaspoon red food coloring
1 teaspoon peppermint extract
1 teaspoon almond extract

In a large bowl, stir together sugar, butter, milk, and egg. Stir in flour, baking powder, and salt. Divide the dough in half. Stir red food coloring and peppermint flavoring into half of the dough. Stir almond flavoring into the other half. Refrigerate 4 to 6 hours.

For each shepherd's staff, shape 1 rounded teaspoon from each of the red dough and white dough. Roll each piece into a 4-inch rope on a floured surface. Place one red rope and one white rope side by side, press together gently, and then twist. Place on ungreased cookie sheet. Curve top down to form a staff.

Bake at 425 degrees F. for 9 to 12 minutes. Cool on wire rack for 30 minutes.

Later, we gather in a circle and hand a candle to each person there. One person lights a candle and shares what the Savior means to him or her. Once the first person is finished, he or she lights the candle of the next person, and it is that person's turn to share. When our children were younger, their thoughts consisted of only a few words: "He is kind," or "I know He loves me." As they became older, the feelings they shared became more personal.

On that evening, as we watch the candles burn down, we take some time to talk about our belief in Jesus Christ and to share examples of the times in the previous year when we have seen His hand in our life. As the flames dance and light up the dark, our own witness burns within, creating a memory that we will be able to look back on and remember. This tradition offers a moment of reflection and dedication. It is a time when we can learn from the example of the shepherds to come closer to Christ, now and with haste, and then share our testimony with others.

TESTIFY

A Christmas Hymn

"Far, Far Away on Judea's Plains"

A Story to Tell . . . A Lesson to Share

Read Luke 2:15–18

Discuss the lessons of the shepherd. Talk about the importance of turning to Christ now, and with haste. What can we learn from the shepherds' relationship with each other when they spoke "one to another" and went as a group to find the Lord? Consider the significance of sharing your testimony of the Savior. What does Jesus Christ mean to you?

The Moment of Celebration

Find a moment to gather together with family or close friends. Let every person make a shepherd's staff from the candy cane cookie recipe. After the cookies have baked, gather everyone into a circle. Light a candle and take an opportunity to share with each other your testimony of Jesus Christ and the moments when you have seen His hand in your life. When everyone has had a turn, place the shepherd figurine in your nativity scene.

THE SHEPHERD

symbolizes a testimony within,

an inner conviction that we have come to know Jesus Christ.

The shepherd is a reminder for us to come closer to the Lord,

now and with haste,

and then to share our testimony with others.

Go and search diligently for the young child.

MATTHEW 2:8

five

THE WISE MEN

One November morning I received a phone call from a friend who was bursting with enthusiasm over a Christmas tradition she had just heard about. "You won't believe it," she told me, "but the children in this family receive only three gifts on Christmas morning. Just three gifts! Isn't that amazing?"

A detailed explanation followed her outburst. Inspired by the knowledge that the Christ child received just three gifts—gold, frankincense, and myrrh, one brilliant mother decided to simplify her Christmas giving. She began by researching the meaning behind the three gifts. Gold was a gift for a king, celebrating the baby's royalty. Myrrh, a common incense used for cleaning and for burial, was given in remembrance of His humanity and foreshadowed the importance of His death. Frankincense, an incense used in the temple, represented His divinity. After studying at great length, this mother decided her gift giving would follow this same pattern. On Christmas morning each gift her children opened would be inspired by the three gifts of the Magi.

I was instantly intrigued. Already on my quest to fill Christmas with Christ, here was a way to simplify and bring meaning to our gift giving. It is a tradition that continues in our home today. On Christmas morning each of my children receives a gift from Santa, and then three other gifts inspired from the gifts of the Magi—one that is joyful, one that is needful, and one that is meaningful. This gift-giving idea has simplified our Christmas mornings and allowed us to really focus on what we are giving, and why. In their simplicity, the gifts have become more personal and more meaningful.

When our children were young, they loved to hear us explain how they were receiving three gifts just as the baby Jesus did. Somehow that comparison drew their hearts closer to Christ on Christmas morning. We have celebrated Christmas this way for more than a decade. I cannot remember a Christmas morning when opening our gifts has not sparked a reminder of Him. Choosing to do things another way helped us to discover Christ—not only in our traditions, but in our celebrations, too.

This is just one of the many lessons we can learn from the wise men. Studying their experience teaches us even more. The account of their journey leads us to believe that it was a privilege for them to search to know the Lord. From the wise men, we learn the importance of understanding the prophecies in the scriptures and being willing to watch carefully for signs of the Savior. Another lesson can be found in the message of this familiar quote, "Wise men still seek Him," which reminds us of the importance of *always* searching to know the Lord. But there is one important lesson we sometimes overlook. Do you remember what happened after the wise men found the Lord? In an effort to ensure the child's safety, and in order to avoid Herod, the wise men returned home another way.

They journeyed another way.

In a world filled with the hustle and bustle of the season, we often find ourselves pulled in many different directions, none of which leads us to Christ. Only the wisest are inclined to journey another way—a way that will protect their belief in Christ.

The wise men remind us of our search to know the Lord, and how sometimes we have to journey another way to come closer to Him. Just like the wise men, the journey may not be what we had originally planned; rather it is what we feel inspired to do. This season, try to find a way to do things differently. You might reconsider your gift giving. Perhaps you will add a new tradition. Maybe you could make a change in your habits or lifestyle that will bring you closer to Him.

This year, follow the example of the Magi and do something another way.

JOURNEY ANOTHER WAY

A Christmas Hymn

"With Wondering Awe"

A Story to Tell . . . A Lesson to Share

Read Matthew 2:1–12

Discuss the lessons of the wise men. Focus on the privilege of their search and their ability to be spiritually sensitive. Talk about their journey and what it means to journey another way.

The Moment of Celebration

This Christmas season try to discover a way to protect your belief in Jesus Christ—one that will allow that belief to grow. Be led to do something differently. Find a new way of celebrating that will lead your family closer to Christ. Search for Him within your Christmas celebrations. Here are some ideas you might want to consider:

- Visiting a live nativity.
- Attending a Christmas concert.
- Participating in a Messiah sing-in.
- Visiting a light display.

It doesn't matter what you choose to do, as long as it leads you closer to Christ. Focus on what you feel and follow those promptings as you try to journey another way. Once you have accomplished your journey, place the wise men in your nativity scene.

THE WISE MEN

exemplify the journey each of us takes as we seek Jesus.

They remind us that as we draw closer to Him,

we will be led to continue our journey another way.

Ye shall find the babe . . . lying in a manger.

Luke 2:12

six

THE LAMB

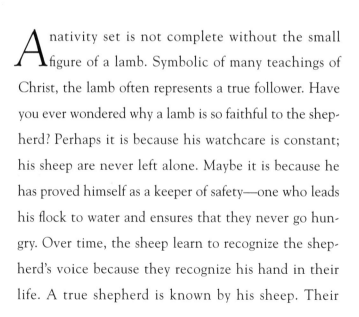

Anativity set is not complete without the small figure of a lamb. Symbolic of many teachings of Christ, the lamb often represents a true follower. Have you ever wondered why a lamb is so faithful to the shepherd? Perhaps it is because his watchcare is constant; his sheep are never left alone. Maybe it is because he has proved himself as a keeper of safety—one who leads his flock to water and ensures that they never go hungry. Over time, the sheep learn to recognize the shepherd's voice because they recognize his hand in their life. A true shepherd is known by his sheep. Their following him becomes a symbol of their gratitude for his devotion.

A dear friend of mine once told me she had looked up synonyms for the word *gratitude* in the dictionary. She found words such as *appreciation*, *indebtedness*, *thanks*, and *acknowledgment*. Then she looked up the verbs that went with gratitude. Two phrases immediately stood out to her. One was "fall to your knees," and the other was "never forget." I find it interesting that those two actions are familiar symbols of worship for those who are true followers of Christ.

The Christmas story is filled with gratitude and thanksgiving—angels praising God (Luke 2:13), shepherds glorifying and praising God (Luke 2:20), and wise men who rejoiced (Matthew 2:10). The scriptural account of the nativity includes more than one fall-to-your-knees moment. These sacred moments have been carefully recorded, never to be forgotten. But within the sacred account found in Luke 2, two characters are mentioned who are often overlooked—Simeon and Anna.

I often find myself pondering why their simple stories are so often left out when the Christmas story is read, and I have wondered on numerous occasions why their figurines are not found in any nativity collections. Simeon and Anna's stories are similar, and they play an important role in the celebration of the birth of Christ. The lessons contained within each are almost repetitive—one right after the other—each a powerful reminder of how we can become true followers of the Good Shepherd, what we need to do to prepare our hearts to recognize Him, and the gratitude that comes in that instant.

Simeon was an older man who was just and devout. He had been promised that he would not die before seeing Christ, and his heart was filled with that longing. It was the Spirit that prompted him to go to the temple on the day Mary and Joseph came to present their son to the Lord. It was there that he discovered the Christ child, and "he took Him in his arms and burst into rapt thanksgiving."[15]

What can we learn from Simeon? Three life-changing lessons: He longed to know Christ, he responded to the promptings of the Spirit, and, in the very instant he recognized the Christ child, he expressed gratitude immediately. We too can follow Simeon's example—we can long to know Christ and prepare so that He will be instantly recognizable, we can feel closer to Christ as we respond to the promptings of the Spirit, and we can remember to express gratitude in those moments when we see His hand in our lives.

Anna, a widow of great age, was also in the temple on that day. Having been widowed for eighty-four years, she had led a life of mourning. We are told that she never left the temple, in fact, "it was her constant and loved resort."[16] Anna's days were filled with service to God and much fasting and prayer. Just like Simeon, "deepest in her soul was longing."[17] Service, prayer, and fasting had prepared her heart to receive Jesus. On that day, filled with inspiration, she, like Simeon, was able to recognize Christ, and "in that instant gave thanks" (Luke 2:38).

Both Simeon and Anna were true followers of Christ. They had prepared their hearts to instantly recognize Him. Both knew how to receive and act on promptings from the Spirit, and they both expressed humble gratitude for the testimony they had been given. I love that their recognition was instant and that their gratitude was immediate. Their stories must not be overlooked; the lessons are far too valuable. From them we learn the importance of gratitude within the celebration.

For Christmas one year my mom gave our family a Tender Mercy Tree and small Tender Mercy journals—one for everyone in the family. The tree held rolled-up scrolls of paper tied with ribbon. A scripture had been carefully typed on each scroll as a reminder for us to watch for the hand of the Lord in our lives and to recognize His tender mercies, or gentle works of grace, all around us. Each evening we would gather together and unroll one of the small scrolls. After someone read the scripture, we took a moment to reflect on the events of the day. We tried to focus on a moment when we had experienced grace in the form of a tender mercy from the Lord during the day. We remembered to look for tender mercies that had been extended to us through the hands of others. Then we wrote our feelings of gratitude in our

Tender Mercy journals. In that instant, we gave thanks. The journals became a reminder of our gratitude and allowed us to prepare our hearts for the season.

Perhaps you might consider finding ways to add more gratitude to your Christmas traditions this year.

I don't think it is a coincidence that Thanksgiving comes before Christmas on the calendar. I believe that a season of gratitude always precedes a season of giving. Gratitude prepares our hearts. Within the memory of our blessings we begin to realize how much we truly have to give. But gratitude can also prepare our hearts in a different way—it can help us recognize Christ.

Expressing our gratitude helps us become true followers of Christ—followers who instantly recognize His hand in our lives. As you strive to fill your heart with gratitude this season, consider the message found in a familiar hymn. As we gather together to offer a prayer of thanksgiving we are gently reminded, "He forgets not His own."[18] The Good Shepherd is aware of us, and He has great blessings in store for us. None of us will be forgotten by the Lord; each of us will have the opportunity to experience miracles from Him. As we look back over our lives, we should remember those fall-to-your-knees moments with gratitude. The simple stories of Simeon and Anna can help remind us to make room for gratitude in the midst of our celebrations. Simeon and Anna were true followers of Christ. Humble and faithful servants, they were as sheep, and recognized their shepherd because they knew His voice (see John 10:4). Although the figures of Simeon and Anna are not found in any nativity sets, use the lamb to represent Simeon and Anna, who recognized the Shepherd and followed Him with grateful hearts.

GIVE THANKS

A Christmas Hymn

"Prayer of Thanksgiving"

A Story to Tell . . . A Lesson to Share

Read Luke 2:25–38

Consider the lessons of Simeon and Anna. How can we prepare our hearts to recognize Jesus Christ? What are some ways that would help to make our recognition instant and our gratitude immediate? How does becoming a true follower of Christ help us to become one of His sheep?

The Moment of Celebration

Create a Tender Mercy Tree. Print out the scriptures listed on the following pages and roll them up into scrolls to place on your tree. Read one scripture each night.

Ponder on a tender mercy in your life that the Lord has given you. Take a moment to record your thoughts. Consider starting a Tender Mercy journal.

Another idea is to find a white stocking to hold your written thoughts. Throughout each day for a week, notice the tender mercies in your life, write them down, and fill the stocking with those thoughts. After reflecting on those mercies, have a private prayer of thanks.

When you are through, place the figure of the lamb in the stable.

TENDER MERCY
SCRIPTURE SCROLLS

2 Corinthians 1:3

"Blessed be God, even the Father of our Lord Jesus Christ, the Father of mercies, and the God of all comfort."

Write down an experience where you have felt comforted by the Lord.

Psalm 145:9

"The Lord is good to all: and his tender mercies are over all his works."

Is there a specific moment in your life when you have realized the goodness of the Lord? Could you make a list of the good things that are in your life?

Psalm 119:156

"Great are thy tender mercies, O Lord."

Sometimes what we think of as a coincidence is really a tender mercy from the Lord. When was the last time you experienced a tender mercy from the Lord? What was it?

Psalm 119:77

"Let thy tender mercies come unto me."

As you pray, ask that your eyes will be open to see the tender mercies from the Lord in the ordinary details of your life this week. Try to remember to write down the ones you recognize.

Psalm 69:16

"Hear me, O Lord; for thy lovingkindness is good: turn unto me according to the multitude of thy tender mercies."

Make a list of the characteristics of the Lord that remind you of His lovingkindness.

Psalm 40:11

"Withhold not thou thy tender mercies from me, O Lord: let thy lovingkindness and thy truth continually preserve me."

Can you remember a time when the tender mercies of the Lord have helped you overcome something you couldn't have handled on your own?

Psalm 103:2, 4

"Bless the Lord, O my soul . . . Who crowneth thee with lovingkindess and tender mercies . . ."

Express gratitude for the multitude of tender mercies that you have recognized from the Lord.

Psalm 25:6

"Remember, O Lord, thy tender mercies and thy loving-kindnesses; for they have been ever of old."

Do you see a pattern of tender mercy experiences in your life? How does recognizing that pattern make you feel?

Luke 1:78

"Through the tender mercy of our God; whereby the dayspring from on high hath visited us, to give light to them that sit in darkness, and in the shadow of death, to guide our feet into the way of peace."

Have you ever experienced a tender mercy in which you felt guided or received light or inspiration to help you move forward? Write that experience down so that you will always remember it.

James 5:11

"Behold, we count them happy which endure. Ye have . . . seen the end of the Lord; that the Lord is very pitiful, and of tender mercy."

How have the Lord's tender mercies helped you endure difficult times?

THE LAMB

*reminds us to prepare our hearts to recognize
the hand of the Lord in our life,
and then, in that instant, to give thanks.*

For unto you is born this day . . . a Saviour,
which is Christ the Lord.

Luke 2:11

seven

THE CHRIST CHILD

In the first few years of our marriage we did not own a nativity set. It was something I always wanted but could never afford. So one year I worked a small job for several afternoons to save up some money for a simple crèche. I bought a very inexpensive set that came with a small wooden stable. The figurines portrayed children dressed up in nativity clothes; they were about three inches tall and made of white porcelain. I chose that particular set because we had two small boys—Caleb, who was three, and Josh, who was just over a year old.

I brought the nativity home and carefully set it up

on the end table in our living room. Josh was too little to notice it, but Caleb was immediately drawn to the new display. I patiently explained to him how fragile each piece was and that he must not touch it, but only look at it with his eyes. I took a moment to point out Joseph with his shepherd's crook, and Mary standing beside the cradle that held the baby Jesus. There was a tiny angel, three wise men, and a shepherd with two tiny lambs. I carefully placed each figure in its appropriate spot—Joseph, Mary, and the baby in the stable, the wise men on the left, and the shepherd and the angel on the right. Then Caleb and I sat back and proudly admired our new decoration.

The next morning Caleb beat me down the stairs. I heard him in the pantry putting Cheerios in a cup to eat while he watched a TV show as I finished getting ready for the day. About fifteen minutes later I followed him down, pausing to look at my new treasure on my way into the kitchen. I was surprised to find it in complete disarray! All of the figurines had been squished together into the stable. There seemed to be no rhyme or reason in their placement, and I knew Caleb must have been involved.

I carefully placed each figure back into its appointed place and went to get Caleb. Again we sat in front of the manger as I patiently explained how important it was not to touch the glass figures because they might break. "We can't touch it," I told him again, "we just look at it." Caleb was such an obedient child—he always had been—and I knew it would not happen again.

Imagine my surprise when I walked down the stairs the next morning and found the scene in the same disarray as the morning before. This time I went right in and got Caleb. Setting him in front of the displaced nativity, I asked, "Did you touch the manger?"

He looked up at me with his round blue eyes and replied, "Yes."

"Do you remember you're not supposed to touch Mommy's manger?" I asked.

Again the reply was the same, "Yes."

"Then why did you touch it?" I questioned.

"Because they can't see Jesus," was his simple reply.

I looked carefully at the manger and realized that perhaps there *was* some order to the disarray. His clumsy little hands had tried to place every figure in a circle around the most important piece of the set—the baby in the manger. Crowded into the small stable, each had a perfect view of the baby. Everyone could see Jesus.

It was a profound lesson.

Needless to say, our display remained that way for the rest of the season, and has every year since then. Interestingly, once each of the figures had been carefully placed in a circle around the baby, Caleb never touched the set again. He was content with the arrangement. The most important figure had become the focus.

Where is your focus this Christmas season?

Can you see Jesus?

I hope He has become the focus of your celebration, the reason for the season, the center of your Christmas beliefs. As Christ becomes our focus, we will begin to realize that Christmas is more than a date on the calendar—it is a way of living. Our hearts can be filled with Christmas every day if we would give as He would have us give, if we would live as He would have us live. I love a poem by Howard Thurman:

THE WORK OF CHRISTMAS

When the song of the angels is stilled,
When the star in the sky is gone,
When the kings and princes are home,
When the shepherds are back with their flock,
The work of Christmas begins:
To find the lost,
To heal the broken,
To feed the hungry,
To release the prisoner,
To rebuild the nations,
To bring peace among brothers,
To make music in the heart.[19]

The poem reminds us that what Jesus Christ gives us does not require money, it requires the heart. As we fill our lives with the work of Christmas, we will find ourselves living the lesson Caleb taught. We will help others to see Christ.

My mother-in-law has a wonderful tradition that we participate in on Christmas Day. We gather as a family and take a moment to think about the upcoming year. Then she hands a piece of paper to each of us and we write down a gift we want to give to Jesus. The gift is something we commit to work on—a goal that will bring us closer to Christ. When we are finished, she hands each of us the white envelope that contains our paper from the previous year. Before placing our new piece of paper into the envelope, we review last year's paper. It gives us a moment to reflect on how we have done and to consider if we have really journeyed closer to Christ. The tradition helps us to focus on Christ, to recognize Him in the midst of our celebrations, and to pause for a moment and remember that *He* is the giver of every good gift.

It helps us see Christ.

BELIEVE

A Christmas Hymn

"Joy to the World"

A Story to Tell . . . A Lesson to Share

Read Luke 2:11–12

The greatest Christmas gift ever given was wrapped in swaddling clothes. Consider what that gift means to you. How has your life been blessed because of the birth of Christ? What are some of the gifts He gives?

The Moment of Celebration

You might consider gathering for this tradition before you open gifts on Christmas morning or as the last thing you do on Christmas Eve. Take a moment to read the Christmas story found in Luke 2. Then, spend a quiet moment pondering what your gift to Christ could be.

Consider some of the things you could work on throughout the year that would help you draw closer to Him. Choose one and write it down. Place it in a white envelope and put it somewhere for safekeeping until next year. Don't forget to open it a year from now and see how well you have done. Once you have written down your gift and sealed it in the envelope, place the last figure in your nativity scene—the Christ child. The most important part of Christmas. The reason for the celebration.

THE CHRIST CHILD

reminds us to offer a gift to the Lord this Christmas season:

A gift based on the true work of Christmas,

one that will allow us to focus on Christ all year long.

WITHIN CHRISTMAS, CHRIST IS FOUND

This is the day of His birth,

Believe it.

This is His gift,

Embrace it.

This is His celebration,

Cherish it.

This is His holiday,

Honor it.

SEVEN NATIVITY TRADITIONS

Mary

*reminds us that we need to find a moment
to ponder the events of that sacred night in Bethlehem.
In that moment we celebrate the miracle of Christ's birth,
and the gift that Heaven gave.*

Joseph

*represents the desires of our hearts.
He reminds us of the secret acts of Christmas kindness
given with sacrifice and love
to the broken, the weary, the lost, or the lonely.*

The Angel

*embodies a heart that runneth over
with the good tidings and great joy of the season.
The angel is a reminder that the anticipation of good things to come
should fill our hearts with warmth overflowing.*

The Shepherd

*symbolizes a testimony within,
an inner conviction that we have come to know Christ.
The shepherd is a reminder for us to come closer to the Lord,
now and with haste,
and then to share our testimony with others.*

The Wise Men

*exemplify the journey each of us takes as we seek Jesus.
They remind us that as we draw closer to Him,
we will be led to continue our journey another way.*

The Lamb

*reminds us to prepare our hearts to recognize
the hand of the Lord in our life,
and then, in that instant, to give thanks.*

The Christ Child

*reminds us to offer a gift to the Lord this Christmas season:
A gift based on the true work of Christmas,
one that will allow us to focus on Christ all year long.*

NOTES

1. Elaine S. McKay, "The Widow's Might," *The Relief Society Magazine*, December 1970, 898–99, written as a tribute to Elizabeth "Bessie" McKay. Author revisions, July 2010.

2. Norman Vincent Peale, "A Gift from the Heart," *Reader's Digest*, January 1968. Reprinted with permission from Reader's Digest. Copyright © 1968 by the Reader's Digest Association, Inc.

3. Chris Van Allsburg, *The Polar Express* (Boston: Houghton Mifflin, 1985).

4. Alfred Edersheim, *The Life and Times of Jesus the Messiah* (New York: E. R. Herrick & Company, 1904), 187–88.

5. Alexander V. G. Allen, *Life and Letters of Phillips Brooks*, vol. 2 (New York: E. P. Dutton and Company, 1901), 49.

6. Edmund H. Sears, "It Came upon the Midnight Clear."

7. Joseph Mohr, "Silent Night."

8. "Oh, Come, All Ye Faithful," attributed to John F. Wade.

9. "Away in a Manger," author unknown.

10. "Angels We Have Heard on High," French carol.

11. Phillips Brooks, "O Little Town of Bethlehem."

12. Ibid.

13. "O Come, O Come, Emmanuel," author unknown. Translated into English in 1851 by John Mason Neale.

14. Philips Brooks, *Christmas Songs and Easter Carols* (New York: E. P. Dutton, 1903), 12.

15. Edersheim, 199.

16. Ibid., 200.

17. Ibid.

18. "Prayer of Thanksgiving," author unknown.

19. Howard Thurman, "The Work of Christmas," in *The Mood of Christmas and Other Celebrations* (Richmond, IN: Friends United Press, 1985), 23.

ACKNOWLEDGMENTS

With thanks and appreciation to the many creative people who worked behind the scenes on this project, including Emily Watts, Malina Grigg, Richard Erickson, and Sheryl Dickert Smith. It is your finishing touches that turn simple words on a page into a journey worth experiencing. Thanks to Jay Ward for the cover and the illustrations—they are just what I had hoped for. Deepest gratitude to Jana Erickson and Chris Schoebinger for your guidance and your vision. Heartfelt thanks to the circle of friends and family who helped in preparation of this book, including the Allens, Apsleys, Bishops, Beardalls, Belchers, Bowens, Bringhursts, Labrums, Mathenys, Morrisons, Murphys, Nortons, Oswalds, Smiths, Vincents, Walkers, and Weeks. And last, but most important, to my family—for loving our Christmas traditions.

ABOUT THE AUTHOR

Emily Belle Freeman's writing reflects a deep love of the scriptures and a strong desire to share their application in modern-day life. She is the author of many books, including, most recently, *The Peter Potential: Discover the Life You Were Meant to Live*. Emily and her husband, Greg, are the parents of four children and live in Lehi, Utah.